GW01464200

CASH AND CARRIE

Plays by the Same Author

Jacobson's Organ

Nigel's Wrist

Cash and Carrie

Nicholas Corder

J. Garnet Miller

First published by J. Garnet Miller
(A division of Cressrelles Publishing Company Limited)
10 Station Road Industrial Estate, Colwall, Near Malvern, WR13 6RN
Telephone/Fax: (01684) 540154

A CIP record for this book is available from the British Library.

ISBN: 0-85343-640-1

Printed in the UK by Cressrelles Publishing Company Ltd.

Characters

Nigel Struthers -
a postgraduate student, who received his doctorate the previous
day. Mid-twenties.

Caroline -
a young actress of similar age; well-spoken and irrepressible.

Scene

The action takes place in the bedroom of Nigel's small flat and is continuous. Surprisingly, he keeps it pretty neat. There is a bed and a few other items of furniture as is felt necessary, including a chair and a small table. There is also a red sports bag and a pink cardigan in the middle of the floor. The "kitchen" and "bathroom" do not have to be incorporated into the set.

Costume

Nigel - Boxer shorts, pink cardigan, dressing-gown.
Caroline - Knickers, a shirt.

Properties

A sports bag (the script refers to it as being red, but obviously this can be altered), containing the following items: bag of cocaine, jockstrap, gaudy necktie, revolver (a magnum 44 is best), 30 bundles of money; 2 mugs of tea; a tea bag.

Act I

Music - Morning Has Broken *by Cat Stevens*
Nigel wakes up hungover. He levers himself carefully out of bed.
Dressed only in boxers, he delicately walks towards the bathroom but,
being a bit cold, he picks up an item of clothing from the floor. It is a
pink cardigan, which he proceeds to put on, unaware of what it is.
Nigel exits to the toilet. We hear appropriate noises from offstage.

Caroline emerges from the far side of the bed. She is dressed in one of
his shirts. She sits up in bed, wide awake and full of life.
Toilet flushes off and Nigel re-enters. He gets back into bed, pulling the
bed-clothes over himself, without noticing Caroline.

Caroline is amused that he has simply settled back down. She bounces up
and down on the bed a few times until he eventually reacts, feels behind
his back and realises that there is someone else in the bed. He leaps out.
Nigel: Oh, my God. Oh, my God. A woman!
                    Caroline beams at Nigel.
Caroline: Morning, Nigel.
Nigel: What . . . ? Who . . . ? How . . . ? Did we . . . ?
Caroline (*Brightly*): Are we going to have a quiz?
Nigel: What are you doing here?

1

Caroline: I'm the official mattress tester from *Slumberland*. They sent me over to check out the bed. *(She bounces up and down a couple of times.)* Bit hard, but reasonably comfortable all the same.

Nigel: What are you doing in my bed?

Caroline: I'd broken the chair and eaten the porridge, so there was nothing left to do but lie down, Baby Bear. What are you doing in my cardigan?

Nigel: What? Oh, my God.

*Nigel looks down and realises he's wearing her cardigan. He whips it off, then realises that he is topless and covers his nipples with his hands. He then notices that **Caroline** is wearing his shirt.*

Nigel: That's my shirt!

Caroline: You said I could wear it, Dr Struthers.

Nigel: I did?

Caroline: Don't you remember?

Nigel: Remember what?

Caroline: About the shirt?

Nigel: The shirt?

Caroline: I'll take it off if you want.

*Caroline moves to take the shirt off and **Nigel** hurriedly stops her.*

Nigel: No, no, it's fine. You wear it.

Caroline: But it's your shirt.

Nigel: No, no. I don't need it. It suits you. Yes. It looks much better on you than it does on me.

Nigel finds his dressing gown and puts it on.

Caroline: You said I could wear it when you promised me breakfast.

Nigel: I did?

Caroline: You said we could have bacon and eggs and fresh buttered toast served up on a tray with steaming fresh coffee and a bud vase containing a single blood-red rose to bring a bloom to my pale, early-morning cheeks.

Nigel: I did?

Caroline: You said that you would squeeze fresh oranges into a cut-glass jug and float paper-thin slivers of kiwi fruit like lily fronds across its golden surface.

Nigel: I did?

Caroline: You said that beauty deserved only the most beautiful of breakfasts. It sounded fabulous. I'm not hungry yet, though. But I could murder a cup of tea.

Nigel: Tea. Yes, I can make tea.

Nigel moves towards the kitchen, which is just off the bedroom.

Caroline: You were wonderful last night.

Nigel: I was?

Nigel exits to kitchen with a bit of a swagger.

Caroline: Yes, my bad back's a lot better now.

Nigel *(Off)*: Bad back?

Caroline: Oh yes. My back was terrible.

Nigel *(Off)*: It's better now, though? A firm mattress helps.

Caroline: It wasn't the mattress, it was the breast re-alignment.

Nigel: What?

Nigel re-enters with a teabag.

Caroline: Breast re-alignment. I'd never heard of it.

Nigel: That's what I thought you said.

Caroline: Yes, I never realised that bi-polar magnetic pull on the breasts was such a common cause of a bad back.

Nigel: Bi-polar?

Caroline: But realigning them has made it loads better.

Nigel: I re-aligned them for you?

Caroline: Although I am beginning to get the odd twinge again. Perhaps you could do it again?

Nigel: *Again? Me?*

Caroline: Yes, you did it so well last time.

Nigel: You're not my patient.

Caroline: I wasn't last night, either. OK, I'm ready.

Nigel: I'm sure you can do them yourself.

Caroline: It didn't look that easy.

Nigel: Just copy what I did. You'll be fine.

Caroline: But I can't remember exactly what you did.

Nigel: It's not that hard.

Caroline: No? It took four goes before you remembered.

Nigel: Well, I suppose . . . I . . . I think that's the kettle.

Nigel scampers off to kitchen.

Caroline: It was fun wasn't it?

Nigel *(Off)*: The realignment?

Caroline: Arabella's party.

Nigel *(Off)*: Arabella?

Caroline: You know Arabella.

Nigel *(Off)*: I don't. I don't know anybody called Arabella.

Caroline: You must do. Everyone knows Arabella.

Nigel *(Pokes head round door)*: Well, I don't. I don't move in the kinds of circles where women are called Arabella. Women I know are called Susan or Joanne. One or two men I know might slap on mascara, Immac their legs and call themselves Arabella on alternate weekends, but I'm not sure if that counts, and even if it did, I still don't get invited to their parties. *(Back to kitchen.)* And even if I did, I wouldn't go.

Caroline: Arabella. Old Carrot Top, we call her.

Nigel *(Off)*: Now don't tell me - I've got it - she's the one with ginger hair.

Caroline: You see, I said you knew her.

Nigel *(Off)*: Milk and sugar?

Caroline: Milk, no sugar please. And don't tell me I'm sweet enough as it is, or I'll be forced to shoot you. *(Nigel re-enters carrying two mugs of tea.)* I've got a deadly eye and a hand like a rock.

*Nigel hands a mug at arm's length to **Caroline**, who sits up in bed to take it off him.*

Nigel: Perhaps you should see a doctor.

Caroline: Perhaps. Ahh, the best china, I see. *(She blows on it and takes a slurp.)* Gosh, this would tickle old Arabella.

*Nigel sits on a chair at some distance from **Caroline**.*

Nigel: Who exactly is this Arabella?

Caroline: Where to start? Arabella? Arabella is a sacred cow, a curator of human beings and a thrower of wild parties.

Nigel: And was it wild?

Caroline: Wild? It was savage! Arabella's main thing is that she collects people. Arabella doesn't work. Daddy owns large tracts of Kensington and half of Scotland. Arabella doesn't have to work. She once did one of those mindless "It girl" columns for

4

the society section of a Sunday newspaper. You know, where they tell everyone about all the posh parties they go to and all the designer brands they wear.

Nigel: I can't say it's the first part of the paper I look at.

Caroline: She likes to show me off to her posh mates as "my friend Caroline:the actress. Caroline's been in *The Bill*, you know." It doesn't occur to her that everyone on the planet with an Equity card's been in *The Bill*.

Nigel: So why's she got a thing about actresses?

Caroline: We call ourselves "actors", Nigel.

Nigel: Actors?

Caroline: I'm not sure. Maybe she likes to think she'll know someone before they get famous. Maybe she envies people who've got drive and determination. You don't have to have much of that when Daddy's put you on an allowance the size of a Bond movie budget.

Nigel: You need drive and determination to be an actress?

Caroline: Actor. And don't get sniffy. I've been building up to this all my life. When all the other kids were handing in their geography projects on time, I was slapping my thighs as Cinderella on a freezing stage in the village hall. I got bruises the shape of my own hand on my legs and fingerprints on my arse from the wanker who thought it was funny to touch up the young girls. He was a church warden, too. I've done all sorts of things just to get on. Arabella's parties are just part of it. I even slept with a theatre director to get one part.

Nigel: Good God, does that still go on?

Caroline: Not as often as they'd like. Although I drew the line at re-enacting the pat of butter scene from *Last Tango* with him.

Nigel: I'm not surprised.

Caroline: You know, the one where Marlon Brando . . .

Nigel: I know the one, there's no need to go into detail. I've seen a lot of films.

Caroline: Me too.

Nigel: I spent my childhood glued to the television watching every film that came on.

Caroline: So did I. The Westerns were the best. My Dad collected hand-guns and I always thought I'd be someone like Calamity Jane, toting one of Dad's revolvers.

Nigel: That's a bit scary. My mother wouldn't even let me have a pen-knife.

Caroline: And now they'll let you perform surgery! You are funny, wandering around drunk with a bag of surgical implements.

Nigel: What?

Caroline (*Indicates the sports bag*)**:** The red bag. You nearly forgot it. I brought it back for you.

Nigel: That's not mine. I've never seen it before in my life.

Caroline: You said it was yours last night. You said it contained the latest in gynaecological equipment. You said I was the only woman you could trust with it.

Nigel: I must have made a mistake.

Caroline: I thought it seemed odd keeping medical stuff in a sports bag. We'd better take a look. Find out whose it is.

Nigel: Are you sure we should?

Caroline: How else are we going to find out who it belongs to? Or perhaps it's like the attaché case in *Pulp Fiction*. Perhaps when you open it, there's just a massive ray of golden light.

Nigel: Or maybe it's the bag with the severed head from *Seven*?

They exchange looks.

Caroline: It's probably got someone's smelly squash kit in it. Go on, open it.

Nigel: You brought it. You open it.

Caroline: You said it was yours, you open it.

Nigel: All right.

*Nigel opens the bag gingerly, puts in a hand
and pulls out a clean jock strap.*

Caroline: Hey! Not a bad guess. Put it on.

Nigel: Don't be silly.

Caroline: Come on. You can pretend to be Malcolm McDowell in *A Clockwork Orange*.

She stares at him in a way that means he can't get out of it.

Nigel (*Slips it on*)**:** Oh, all right, then.

Caroline: Fabulous. You could be his twin brother.

Nigel: "Viddy well, little brother, viddy well." *(He struts around for a bit, singing* Singing in the Rain.*)* Your go.

> *Caroline pulls out a plastic bag full of white powder.*

Nigel: What is it?

Caroline: I don't think it's talcum powder.

Nigel: I don't know. Those jockstraps can rub your bits red raw.

Caroline: Do you think it's what I think?

Nigel: I have no idea. They abandoned Clairvoyance, Spiritualism and Fortune-telling when the Government cut back on the Philosophy Department. Although God knows that economics is more or less the same thing.

Caroline: Cocaine?

Nigel: I've never tried it.

Caroline: Nor me. I can't afford to try it.

Nigel: You wait till you've got a long contract on *Eastenders* or do a Hollywood blockbuster, then it's compulsory.

Caroline: How can you tell if it's cocaine?

Nigel: In the movies, they dip in a finger like a sherbet dab and wipe it around their gums.

Caroline: What does that do?

Nigel: It's what they do in films.

Caroline: Life isn't films, you know. You don't just suddenly come across a stash of cocaine in real life.

Nigel: Cocaine can be very damaging. If you take it for long enough, it can wear a hole through your septum. That's the bit that separates your nostrils.

Caroline: Yuck, that's horrible.

Nigel: Yes, but at least you can pick your nose from the opposite side.

Caroline (*Referring to the bag*): Your turn.

Nigel: I'm not sure I want to play.

> *Caroline pulls out a wodge of used twenty pound notes.*

Caroline: All right, then.

Nigel: Bloody hell. How much is there?

Caroline: They're all twenties. (*Quickly flicking.*) There must be at least fifty of them.

Nigel: A thousand pounds. Who goes around with a bag of cocaine and a thousand pounds? We could be on dangerous ground here. I'm sure that you can't get through this much cocaine for personal use.

Caroline: It's got to belong to a dealer.

Nigel: Do you know any?

Caroline: No, but Arabella's got some odd friends. Come on, let's see what else there is.

> *Caroline goes to dip into the bag, but **Nigel** stops her.*

Nigel: I've changed my mind. I'm back in the game. (*Pulls out an extravagantly coloured tie.*) Oh, great. You get a stash of cocaine and a grand in used notes, I get a second-hand man's wardrobe.

Caroline: Go on, have another go. I don't want you sulking.

Nigel (*Pulls out a gun*): An athletic, wealthy, psychopathic drug dealer with bad taste in ties. This is getting nightmarish.

Caroline: Is it real?

Nigel: It looks real enough to me.

Caroline: Here, let me have a look.

> *Nigel hands the gun to **Caroline**, who examines it very professionally.*

Caroline: You're right.

Nigel: Bloody hell! Be careful.

> *Caroline totes the gun and her mood seems to change instantly.*

Caroline: You've been lying to me, Nigel.

Nigel: What do you mean?

Caroline: You haven't got any bacon and eggs have you?

Nigel: I was going to pop out for some.

Caroline: You haven't got any orange juice either, have you?

Nigel: No, the shop's just round the corner.

Caroline: And that's where you were going to buy the vase and the rose?

Nigel: It's like Aladdin's cave in there - they've got everything.

Caroline: I bet you never even buy Kiwi fruit.

Nigel: Occasionally.

Caroline: Just about everything you said, Nigel, was a fib, a lie, an untruth, a porkie. (*She aims the gun at him and Nigel backs away.*) You're not even a proper doctor, are you Nigel?

Nigel (*Cowering*): Yes, I am.

Caroline: You're not a medical doctor, though, are you?

Nigel: Not precisely.

Caroline: Yes or no, Nigel?

Nigel: I've got a PhD. I've got a doctorate. Most doctors have only got bachelor's degrees – in surgery and medicine. A PhD is a proper doctor.

Nigel backs towards the bed as she appears increasingly menacing.

Caroline: It's not quite the same thing, is it? I mean, a PhD hardly qualifies you to go around feeling up women's breasts now, does it, Nigel?

Nigel: I was drunk. I don't remember.

Caroline: You touched my breasts under false pretences.

Nigel: I only meant it as a bit of fun.

Caroline: No-one knows I'm here, Nigel.

Nigel: What do you mean?

Caroline: I can do anything, and no-one will know.

Nigel: Arabella! Arabella, knows you're here!

Caroline: Who's Arabella, Nigel?

Nigel: The one with the party. Old Carrot Top.

Caroline: But you can't remember her, can you Nigel? You were too drunk. You lied to me. Just to cop a feel of my tits. That's rather sad, don't you think? I'm just going to have to shoot you.

Nigel: Take the bag. Take all of it and go.

Caroline: I intend doing that, Nigel. First, I've got a score to settle.

Nigel: No, please. I've only just got my PhD.

Caroline: I've decided. I am sorry about this, but I'm going to have to shoot you, Nigel.

Nigel: But I'm the country's only authority on contemporary German comic writing. (*Curls himself into a ball, hiding under the duvet, as though it will deflect bullets.*) If I die, all that knowledge goes with me.

Caroline: I don't think the world is going to miss out too much if the Germans stop writing comedy. Too late, Nigel.

Caroline fires five shots. After the gunfire, there is a long moment of silence.

Nigel: I'm not dead.

Caroline (*As Clint Eastwood*): "I know what you're thinking. Did she fire six shots or only five? Well, to tell you the truth, in all this excitement, I've kind of lost track myself. But being as this is a 44 Magnum, the most powerful handgun in the world, and would blow your head clean off, you've got to ask yourself one question - Do I feel lucky? Well, do you punk?"

Nigel raises his head and starts feeling and checking his body for bullet holes.

Nigel: I'm not dead. There's no blood. I'm alive.

Caroline: I'd have thought with your enormous knowledge of film you'd have got the reference, Nigel. *Dirty Harry*?

Nigel: That's not fair!

Caroline: You're the one who claimed to be a film buff. I'd have thought you might have heard of Clint Eastwood. Besides, it's a replica.

Nigel: You said it was real.

Caroline: No, I didn't. You said "It looks real" and I agreed. It does look real. It looks real enough, but it's a fake. Rather like Dr Struthers's breast realignment technique.

Nigel: Well what was all that about?

Caroline: I'm an actress, Nigel. I like pretending. It's fun being someone else from time to time. What's your excuse?

Nigel gets up huffily.

Nigel: You scared the shit out of me.

Caroline: And you felt my tits.

Nigel: I cured your bad back, didn't I?

Caroline: And I got to the truth. Why do you have to pretend you're someone you're not?

Nigel: Isn't that what you do for a living?

Caroline: Touché. But you don't have to pretend, Nigel. There's nothing wrong with you. You've got the brainpower of two people.

Nigel: Yes, I know, Laurel and Hardy.

Caroline: You don't have to make jokes all the time.

Nigel: It's my speciality. After all, I am the German comedy king.

Caroline: I think you'll find Germany is a republic.

Nigel (*Points at gun*): Christ, you had me worried, there.

Caroline: I'm sorry. I couldn't resist it. You're so cute when you're frightened.

Nigel: And I'm not when I'm the fearless doctor?

Caroline: I knew all along you weren't a real doctor.

Nigel: You mean a medical man.

Caroline: I just thought you were the only one at the party who seemed remotely interesting. All the others seemed to be pretending to be something they weren't.

Nigel: That's strange. I thought I was supposed to have pretended to be a medic.

Caroline: You did. Compared to the others, you were so bad at it, it was ... well, I thought it had a certain charm, you know, like a little boy lost.

Nigel: Please don't tell me I brought out the mother in you.

Caroline: And you kept on saying funny things.

Nigel: I'm not surprised. I was drunk. Whatever I said, forget I said it.

Caroline: Why? You were witty, you were flattering. You were poetic.

Nigel: Poetic?

Caroline: Yes, poetic. You said things that made me feel wanted.

Nigel: Like Butch Cassidy and the Sundance Kid?

Caroline: Like a woman.

> **Nigel** *is mildly embarrassed that she has got a little too near his true feelings.*

Nigel: Hey! We've got a bag to investigate.

Caroline: Right.

> *Caroline empties the bag - there are loads more bundles of notes.*

Nigel: Is that it?

Caroline: What do you mean "is that it?", there must be thousands here.

Nigel: I mean, no more bizarre accessories.

Caroline (*Looks inside bag*): No, doesn't look like it.

Nigel: How much do you think there is?

Caroline: There's only one way to find out.

Nigel: Are they all the same?

Caroline (*Examines them*): They all seem to be used £20 notes.

Caroline starts stacking them up quickly.

Nigel: My God! I think there's thirty thousand pounds here.

Caroline: Thirty thousand pounds!

Nigel: Thirty thousand! I'd have to donate sperm fifteen hundred times to make that much.

Caroline: What?

Nigel: It's kind of a paying hobby.

Caroline: What are we going to do with all this?

Nigel: It's too suspicious. Whoever owns this is probably not the kind of person you'd want to mess with.

Caroline: Yes, but who knows we've got this?

Nigel: Arabella?

Caroline: Arabella was away with the fairies. She was in a worse state than you.

Nigel: Didn't anybody say anything?

Caroline: Only you, when you pretended it was your bag.

Nigel: Oh, shit! They're probably out their looking for us right now. Any moment now John Travolta and Samuel L. Jackson are going to come through that door touting uzis and spouting bits of *The Bible*.

Caroline: I don't think anybody saw us.

Nigel: Are you sure?

Caroline: There was nobody else there, by then. Look, if it's Arabella's, it means about the same to her as it does to you if you can't get your quid back out of a supermarket trolley.

Nigel: I'm nervous about this.

Caroline: You're nervous about everything, Nigel. There's a simple solution, we'll split it fifty-fifty.

Nigel: Who gets the cocaine?

Caroline: Do you want it?

Nigel: No.

Caroline: We can always flush it down the loo.

Nigel: Or you could wait till you get a gig on *Eastenders* and flog it then.

Caroline: Or take a stall on Portobello Road.

Nigel: You decide. You keep it. And the gun.

Caroline: Thanks, Nigel. And you can have the tie and jockstrap.

Nigel: You realise that's fifteen thousand pounds each?

Caroline: Fifteen thousand pounds!

Nigel: That's three thousand trips to the cinema, twenty thousand café lattes or half the Manchester City midfield.

Caroline: I could go mad at Gucci, sprinkle cash like confetti in the food halls of Fortnum and Mason, the world is my oyster.

Nigel: Hey! You could invest it in a new play. Create some exciting new sensational work that will take the West End by storm.

Caroline: I'd need more than fifteen grand.

Nigel: I might lend you some of mine.

Caroline: Besides, most new plays are crap. It's because they're written by playwrights.

Nigel: Now there's a thing.

Caroline: Have you ever met a playwright? They're obnoxious little prigs who smell of stale urine. They only write plays because they can't write proper books.

Nigel: Well, do an old play. I understand there's a chap called Shakespeare who's got something of a reputation.

Caroline: They're awful. They sniff round you at parties to see if you're prepared to be in one of their plays, which always require you to get your kit off or fake an orgasm.

Nigel: "You know, you look mighty pretty when you get mad."

Caroline: Thank you, Nigel.

Nigel: It's John Wayne, *The Man Who Shot Liberty Valance.*

Caroline: I know. I recognised it. He says it to Vera Miles. Westerns are one of my specialities, remember. I probably know more about films than you do.

Nigel: I doubt it.

Caroline: What makes you say that?

Nigel: I just absorb things. I don't have to make an effort to memorise things. They just stick.

Caroline: And I'm a trained actor. We have to learn lines. My memory is honed to remember things. If we had a film quiz, I'd win.

Nigel: Let's just agree that we both know a lot about film. It's not something to argue about. Politics, religion and whether Rio Ferdinand is worth £14.5 million per leg. These are things to argue about. Not films.

Caroline: No, come on. You've got a PhD, I've only got six GCSEs. Let's see who knows more. Let's see if you really do know a lot about films. It could be the revenge of the educational under-achiever.

Nigel: Leave it.

Caroline: I bet you a thousand pounds I know more than you do.

Nigel: Where on earth are you going to get a thousand pounds from?

Caroline, smiling, picks up a wad of notes.

Caroline: You're not chicken are you?

Nigel: "Is that meaning me? Chicken? You shouldn't call me that."

Caroline: James Dean – *Rebel Without A Cause*.

Nigel: Very impressive.

Caroline: You see, I might just know more than you think. (*Waves money at him.*) Drugs and money, Nigel. We could make a game of it. "As far back as I remember, I wanted to be a gangster."

Nigel: That's *Goodfellas*. Ray Liotta.

Caroline: Come on, Nigel. You see, you're good at it. But exactly how good? Where's your spirit of adventure? Let's bet.

Nigel: I don't want to. I only like playing games where I know the odds.

Caroline: Stop calculating and start living. I bet you twenty quid you don't know the next film quotation.

Nigel: Twenty quid?

Caroline: Nigel, you've got fifteen thousand pounds sitting right there. What's twenty quid?

Nigel: I never had any money before. It's enough for a down-payment on a flat.

Caroline: And if you won it all, it would be enough for a down-payment on a house.

Nigel: This could be a fresh start for me. For either of us.

Caroline: For both of us.

Nigel *(Weighing up money)***:** It's too much to lose.

Caroline: You didn't have it until a few minutes ago. Be bold. Be adventurous. Put your money where your mouth is.

Nigel: I'm not sure.

Caroline: Just bet.

Nigel: I don't know.

Caroline: "What we've got here is a failure to communicate."

Nigel: We have? Oh, I see. Another movie quote. Strother Martin in *Cool Hand Luke*.

Caroline: I told you you were good. Now just bet the tie and jock-strap to start with. After all, you've already lost your shirt. No matter what happens, I'm keeping this.

Nigel: Fair's fair. All right, I'll bet you the jockstrap, the tie and your pink cardigan.

Caroline: But it's my cardigan.

Nigel: If you're keeping the shirt, the cardigan's mine. I can bet with it if I want. Besides, you can buy a lot of women's knitwear with thirty grand.

Caroline: OK. Off you go.

Nigel: What are you going to bet then?

Caroline: I'll bet you the cocaine.

Nigel: What good is the cocaine to me?

Caroline: If you win back the jockstrap you can dust your privates with it and stop them from getting sore.

Nigel: Right. Who said "You're only supposed to blow the bloody doors off!"?

Caroline: Too easy. Michael Caine – *The Italian Job*. It looks like I've won myself a sparkling array of gentlemen's haberdashery and a lifetime's supply of nose candy.

Nigel stops her from picking up her winnings.

Caroline: What are you doing? I won.

Nigel: Not yet, you haven't.

Caroline: Was it or was it not Michael Caine?

Nigel: Yes.

Caroline: In *The Italian Job*?

Nigel: Of course.

Caroline: Then I've won.

Nigel: Double or quits?

Caroline: All right. A hundred pounds?

Nigel: Twenty!

Caroline: Eighty.

Nigel: Do you have any idea how hard it is to earn twenty quid? All right, forty.

Caroline: Sixty?

Nigel: Forty.

Caroline: OK, forty. *(She throws in two £20 pound notes. Nigel doesn't react.)* Forty pounds each.

Nigel reluctantly peels off two twenties and adds them to the pile.

Caroline: I don't know what we're fighting about. Oh, I know. "Gentlemen, you can't fight in here. This is the War Room."

Nigel: Too easy. Peter Sellers in *Doctor Strangelove*.

Caroline: I'm sorry, that's not its full title. It's *Doctor Strangelove or How I Learned to Stop Worrying and Love the Bomb*.

Nigel: You didn't give me time to finish.

Caroline: That sounds funny coming from a man.

Nigel: Right then. A hundred quid.

Caroline: You're getting daring, Nigel.

Nigel: Come on, a hundred quid. Let's see it.

Nigel slaps down five £20s. Caroline follows suit, but almost like a striptease, licking her finger between peeling off each note.

Caroline: OK, Big Boy, hit me with your best shot.

Nigel hesitates. He's thinking.

Caroline: Come on, come on, I'll have to hurry you.

Nigel: Hang on.

Caroline (*She knows he means "wait", but kids him with*): I don't know. James Stewart in *Vertigo*?

Nigel: No, no, no.

Caroline: Richard Burton on top of the cable car in *Where Eagles Dare*?

Nigel: Hang on!

Caroline: Sylvester Stallone in *Cliffhanger*?

Nigel: No. I haven't thought of one yet.

Caroline (*Pinches his cheek*): Can't little Nigey-wigey think of a question?

Nigel: Leave off. "A boy's best friend is his mother."

Caroline: Is that a quotation, a statement of how you feel, the way you see me, or a combination of all three?

Nigel: It's a quote. "A boy's best friend is his mother."

Caroline: It's got to be a guess, but I'll go for Anthony Perkins in *Psycho*.

Nigel: Correct.

Caroline: Shall we raise the stakes a little?

Caroline throws in the remainder of the wad from which she has been peeling notes.

Nigel: How much was that?

Caroline: Whatever's left over from £1,000. You work it out. You're the clever one. Maths was one of the ones I didn't get.

Nigel: That's a lot.

Caroline: What you've never had, you won't miss.

Nigel (*Throws in remainder of his wad*): I must be barking mad.

Caroline: "My mama always said, life was like a box of chocolates. You never know what you're going to get."

Nigel: Tom Hanks in *Forrest Gump*.

Caroline: There's no fooling the boy. You never know what you're going to get, do you, Nigel? Sometimes we get more than we deserve and every good boy deserves favour. Be good, Nigel!

Nigel: You obviously passed Music, then.

Caroline: Another thousand.

    Caroline throws in her next wad. **Nigel** *slowly does the same.*

Nigel: Is this getting out of hand?

Caroline: Not yet.

Nigel: "I know what gold does to men's souls."

Caroline *(Teasing)*: Don't be so pompous.

Nigel: It's a line from a film. "I know what gold does to men's souls."

Caroline: Oh, it's *The Treasure of the Sierra Madre*. The director's father. John . . . no . . . Walter Huston.

Nigel: You're good.

Caroline: I'm better when I'm bad.

Nigel: Mae West?

Caroline: No, I mean, I'm better when I'm bad.

Nigel: Sometimes, I'm not sure if I understand you.

Caroline: Your thoughts are in your head, Nigel. Try lowering them a couple of feet. Another thousand?

    Caroline throws in a wad, **Nigel** *follows suit.*

Nigel: I think we know who's going to win. "I love the smell of napalm in the morning, smells like – victory!"

Caroline: Not with easy-peasy ones like that you're not. Robert Duvall – *Apocalypse Now*. You're always doing tough guy stuff.

Nigel: You're the one who likes westerns.

Caroline: Do something a little gentler. You know, something that might get a person, if they wanted, in the mood? You can have another go.

Nigel: OK, how about "I've got a head for business and a body for sin."?

Caroline: Melanie Griffiths – *Working Girl*. A bit of sin would make a nice change, Nigel. I'll raise you three.

    Caroline chucks in three thousand. **Nigel,** *getting into the spirit of things now, does the same.*

Nigel: Oh, what the hell!

Caroline: "There are men who think it's their duty to flirt with women."

Nigel: I suppose there must be.

Caroline: You're stalling for time.

Nigel: Is that your quote?

Caroline: Yes. "There are men who think it's their duty to flirt with women."

Nigel: That's a bit of an obscure one, but I think you'll find it's Bette Davis in *The Letter*.

Caroline: Impressive. I didn't think you'd get that. And do you think it's your duty?

Nigel: You're trying to put me off, aren't you? Hoping I'm going to lose concentration. "Here's how you get him. He pulls a knife, you pull a gun. He sends one of yours to the hospital, you send one of his to the morgue."

Caroline: Sean Connery, *The Untouchables*. Five thousand.

Caroline chucks in £5,000. Nigel hesitates, then does the same.

Caroline: "You don't have to say anything and you don't have to do anything. Not a thing. Oh, maybe just whistle. You know how to whistle, don't you, Steve? You just put your lips together and blow."

Nigel whistles. Things are steaming up.

Nigel: Lauren Bacall, *To Have and Have Not*. "I don't know how to kiss, or I would kiss you. Where do the noses go?"

Caroline: I think you'll find that's Ingrid Bergman in *For Whom the Bell Tolls*.

They both throw in the last of their money.

Nigel: Where do we go from here?

Caroline: Let's just see how the game unfolds. *(She moves in close to Nigel.)* "Tu as des beaux yeux, tu sais. You have beautiful eyes, you know." I got an A in my French.

Nigel: Are we allowed foreign films?

Caroline: Did you watch them as well?

Nigel: Yes.

Caroline: Then we're allowed them.

Nigel: But only European.

Caroline: Yes, but no German comedies.

Nigel: Don't worry, there aren't any. I'm an expert.

Caroline: Well who was it, Nigel?

Nigel: Jean Gabin in either *Pépé le Moko* or *Quai des Brûmes*.

Caroline: Which one, Nigel?

Nigel: Pépé ... Quai ... Pépé *(He watches her eyes for a reaction.)* Pépé le Moko.

Caroline: Oh, bad luck.

Nigel: Come on, it was near enough.

Caroline: All right, I'll let you have it if you can tell me what Michèle Morgan says in reply.

Nigel: Oh, it's something really corny! Oh yes, "Embrasse-moi. Kiss me."

Caroline grabs Nigel and kisses him with some force.
Nigel is too stunned to react.

Nigel: What did you do that for?

Caroline: What did you say before?

Nigel: "Embrasse-moi. Kiss me."

Caroline: Exactly. *(She grabs him again and kisses him even more passionately. This time, Nigel responds a little.)* "Is that a pistol in your pocket or are you pleased to see me?"

Nigel: Mae West – *I'm No Angel*.

Caroline: Very good, Nigel. So are you pleased to see me?

Nigel: I'm not sure yet. "You should be kissed and often, and by someone who knows how."

Caroline: Clark Gable, *Gone With The Wind*. So let's try again. *(They kiss again.)* And whilst we're on the subject of kissing. "It's an old custom. All the really high civilisations go for it. It stimulates the whole system. As a matter of fact, you can't be in tip-top health without it."

Nigel: It's from *Forbidden Planet*, but I can't remember who.

Caroline: All right, I'll let you have that one, but only because it might lead somewhere more interesting.

Caroline kisses Nigel, then retreats to the bed and takes up a Mrs Robinson pose, putting one leg provocatively on the bed.

Nigel: "Mrs Robinson, you're trying to seduce me."

Caroline: You're going to have to think of something a little bit more obscure than that. Dustin Hoffman, *The Graduate*. "You want me, you're going to have to come and get me!"

Nigel: Edward G. Robinson – *Little Caesar*. "If this is foreplay, then I'm a dead man."

Nigel throws money into the air, so that the notes settle everywhere.

Caroline: Steve Guttenberg, *Cocoon*.

*Caroline holds back the covers and **Nigel** jumps in.*

Nigel: "For what I am about to receive, may I make myself truly thankful."

Caroline: Peter O'Toole – *The Ruling Class*. "Fill your hands, you son of a bitch!"

They dive under bedclothes. The following takes place under the duvet to accompanying grunts and groans.

Nigel: John Wayne – *True Grit*. "Fasten your seat-belts, kids. It's going to be a bumpy night."

Caroline: Bette Davis – *All About Eve*. "All right! Let's give some empty lives a little meaning!"

Nigel: Steve Martin – *Leap of Faith*. "Is it safe? Is it safe?"

Caroline: Laurence Olivier, *Marathon Man*. "Listen to the children of the night. What music they make."

Nigel: Bela Lugosi – *Dracula*. "Excuse me while I whip this out!"

Caroline: *Blazing Saddles*, Cleavon Little. Little it isn't! "Will you help me get undressed, please?"

Nigel: Audrey Hepburn – *Roman Holiday*. "I'm definitely not wearing my underwear."

Caroline: Dustin Hoffman - *Rain Man*. *(With mounting excitement.)* "Yes, yes, yes, yes, yes, yes, yes, yes!"

Nigel: *When Harry Met Sally* – Meg Ryan. "Hi-ho, Silver."

Caroline: Clayton Moore – *The Lone Ranger*. "Yabba dabba do!"

Nigel: John Goodman – *The Flintstones*.

They finish together.

Nigel: Jesus Christ, that was fantastic!

Caroline: Charlton Heston - *The Greatest Story Ever Told*?

Nigel: No, Nigel Struthers – *Cash and Carrie*!

Music - Sweet Caroline by Neil Diamond.

Curtain